Bed and Breakfast Brilliance

Starting and Operating a Cozy, Profitable Inn

Table of Contents

Chapter 1. Introduction

Dive headfirst into the charming world of bed and breakfasts with "Bed and Breakfast Brilliance: Starting and Operating a Cozy, Profitable Inn." This Special Report, laden with warmth and enthusiasm, immerses you into the fundamentals of opening, running, and reaping success from your very own B&B. No stone is left unturned; from finding the perfect location, understanding zoning laws, to crafting the quintessential breakfast menu that will keep your guests coming back for more. If you've ever longed for a life filled with fresh-baked muffins, bubbling conversations from around the globe and a profitable business you can call your own, this guide will light a spark in your entrepreneurial spirit. Step by step, let's shape your dream into reality - buy this Special Report today and start your delightful venture tomorrow!

Chapter 2. Discovering Your Bed and Breakfast Vision

Every plunging wave begins merely as a ripple on the surface, originating from a surge of energy below. Similarly, the grandest dreams stem from an idea, a vision. As you begin to contemplate the scope and scale of running an enchanting bed and breakfast, the first step is to clarify your vision.

2.1. Understand Your Motive

Your motive behind starting a B&B serves as the foundation of this undertaking. Beyond the desire to own a business or foster hospitality, there may be personal reasons which propel you towards this venture - perhaps a love for meeting new people, a passion for cooking, or a knack for creating a welcoming environment. Identify these motives to strengthen and ground your vision. Remember, a stronger motive equates to a more resilient business as it will weather storms.

2.2. Master the Basics

Before sketching your picture-perfect B&B, one needs a concrete understanding of the basics. Start by familiarizing yourself with the industry particulars and know your marketplace. How do B&Bs differentiate themselves from hotels? What is the predominant clientele? What are the expected services that set a B&B apart? Your preferences and ideas are vital, but to foster success, they must align with the proven staples of bed and breakfast businesses.

2.3. Paint Your B&B Picture

Now that you have understood your motivations and grasped the basics, let your imagination roam freely as you envision the dream B&B. Are you located in a bustling city, offering a peaceful niche amid the urban cacophony, or snuggled away in the tranquil countryside, providing a perfect retreat? Every detail, minute or monumental, from the style of architecture to the color scheme, plays a role in your vision. Sketch this vision, quite literally if possible, to create a representation that you can refer back to and share with others.

2.4. Define The Guest Experience

Contemplate not just the physical aspect of your B&B, but also the experiences you want to offer your guests. Picture a day in the life of your guest, from their arrival to their departure. Detail each feature and service you want to provide. Will they be greeted with a warm cookie and a map of the local sights, or will they receive a more personal tour of the property? Will the breakfast be served individually or will it be a communal affair? Each of these experiences form the unique tapestry of your B&B.

2.5. Your Role as the Host

As the owner of a B&B, you will wear many hats - property manager, head chef, concierge, and above all, the host. Your personal touch will make a difference in setting your B&B apart from others. Reflect on the host you aspire to be - are you the jovial character who jokes with guests over breakfast or the gentle, invisible orchestrator ensuring a flawless stay? Your style of hosting not only affects your guests' experience but also your enjoyment in running the business.

2.6. Financial Overview

While it may seem slightly detached from the creative exercise of defining your vision, having an initial understanding of the financial aspects of running a B&B is integral to shaping a feasible vision. Understand the costs involved - both initial investment and running costs, the prices you can charge based on the services you intend to offer and the expected returns on investment. Your B&B dream should also be financially sustainable. Seek advice, read up on the subject or consult with a mentor in this area to ensure you are on the right track.

2.7. Refine Your Vision

Now that you have a comprehensive vision of your dream B&B, it's time to refine it. Review all aspects and ask yourself - is this feasible? Have you missed out on anything critical, or added in features which, upon reflection, are superfluous? Remember, this vision isn't set in stone. It's fluid, dynamic, and will likely evolve as you proceed on your journey. However, always maintaining a clear vision of your B&B will act as your compass, guiding your decisions and actions in bringing this vision to life.

As you conclude this chapter, remember that the foundation of your bed and breakfast begins with this vision. By determining your motives, understanding the basics, creating a detailed plan, defining your role as a host, and having a financial overview, you can develop a realistic and aspirational vision for your B&B. So, hold onto this vision, nurture it and, step by step, turn it into your splendid reality.

Chapter 3. Choosing the Perfect Location for Your Inn

Choosing the right location for your bed and breakfast is the first, and perhaps the most important step you'll take on your journey to building a successful inn. The location you select will not only determine the initial costs and legal obligations you'll face but will also have a significant impact on your future clientele base and capacity to generate profits.

3.1. Understanding Your Ideal Guest

Before you start searching for potential properties, it's critical to first understand who your ideal guests are. Understanding your target market will guide you in your quest to find the ideal location.

Envision your typical guest. Is she a busy executive looking for a peaceful, quiet weekend getaway? Or is a retired couple seeking to explore hidden gems across the country? Maybe it's the young couple in search of a romantic destination. The answers to these questions will give you clues about what geographical features and local attractions your location must have.

3.2. Geographic Considerations

Once you have a sense of the type of guest you are targeting, you should consider the geographic features that will appeal to this group.

For those seeking to cater to peace and tranquility seekers, serene locations such as mountainsides, lakefronts, and forests make great choices. Access to natural beauty such as national parks, beaches, and recreational activities like hiking, swimming, or bird-watching may be desirable for these guests.

On the other hand, if you wish to draw in couples looking for a romantic getaway, choose a location with attractions such as vineyards, fine dining restaurants, spas, and seclusion from busy city life.

3.3. Proximity to Attractions

Often, the success of a bed and breakfast hinges on its proximity to major tourist attractions. Visitors are generally willing to pay a premium for lodging that is within a short distance of popular sites, or even more so, offers a stellar view of them.

But here's a rule of thumb: the closer your inn is to an attraction, the more dependent your business will be on the seasonality of that attraction. It's a double-edged sword and requires a well thought out business strategy to ensure off-peak periods can be weathered.

Considerations might include:

- Historical or cultural sites
- National parks and nature sanctuaries
- Entertainment hubs and nightlife
- Convention centers
- Popular event venues

3.4. Accessibility

Rural, tucked-away places can be charming locations for a bed and breakfast, but be careful not to understate the importance of accessibility. Your guests should be able to get to your B&B with relative ease. A secluded inn in the middle of nowhere may seem part of the appeal, charming even, but if it's too hard to get to, it could be a blow to your business.

Accessibility doesn't only mean the ease of reaching the premise but also, once there, the presence of parking facilities, the quality of local roads, proximity to public transport, and convenience to the city center or essential shops.

3.5. Zoning Laws and Building Codes

A bed and breakfast must adhere to zoning laws and building codes in your chosen location. Zoning laws regulate how the land in certain areas can be used, and building codes ensure that buildings are safe for occupation.

Before purchasing a property for your bed and breakfast, consult with a local attorney or a city's planning department to ensure the property is zoned appropriately for your intended use. Failure to adhere to these laws can result in costly fines or, worse, requirings you to cease operations completely.

3.6. The Cost Aspect

Last but by no means least, what you can afford plays a crucial role. As the saying goes, "Location, location, location" is everything in real estate - and unfortunately, prized locations come with a heftier price tag. Careful budgeting is necessary to ensure that your entrepreneurial dream doesn't end in a financial nightmare. Remember to consider not only the price of the property but also the cost of any necessary renovations to make it suitable for a bed and breakfast.

In conclusion, selecting the perfect location for your bed and breakfast requires careful consideration of the type of guest you wish to attract, the geographic features that will appeal to such guests, the proximity of the premises to attractions, and the accessibility. Laws of the local municipality and the cost of purchasing and maintaining the location are also essential factors. With careful planning and research, you can land a location that will sow the seeds for your successful B&B venture.

Chapter 4. Understanding Zoning Laws and Regulations

Before starting your Bed and Breakfast (B&B) journey, there's a fundamental step you must take - Understanding Zoning Laws and Regulations. These laws serve to control the way land is used and build upon in certain areas, often with the objective of ensuring the compatibility of adjacent uses and preserving the character of a community.

4.1. Understanding What Zoning Is

Zoning is generally the mechanism by which municipalities control land use and architectural design to prevent conflicting land uses within a community. It is an integral dimension of planning strategy, designed to influence the way land is used and developed.

The primary aim of zoning is to segregate uses that are thought to be incompatible, thereby preventing damage caused by new development to existing properties. For instance, residential properties may be zoned to be separate from commercial or industrial areas.

It's vital to comprehend that zoning laws differ significantly from town to town, city to city, and state to state. Hence, it's crucial never to assume that just because a particular use is acceptable in one area, it will be acceptable in another.

4.2. The Relevance of Zoning Laws to your B&B

Starting a B&B in your home can be an exciting venture, merging your hospitality skills with an available asset - your home. However, whether you can legally operate a B&B in your home depends on your home's zoning. For instance, if your house is located in a purely residential zone, it may be illegal for you to run a B&B because operating a B&B is considered a commercial activity.

Moreover, zoning laws might also dictate what changes you can make to your home. This may extend to structural and aesthetic upgrades for catering to your guests like extending a wing, adding bathrooms, or even more fundamental modifications, like changing the landscaping or modifying your parking.

When you violate zoning laws by operating a Bed and Breakfast without the requisite permissions, there are a variety of possible consequences, such as: - Legal suits filed by neighbors or the municipality - Heavy fines or penalties - Requirement to cease operations - Devaluing of your property

Above all, the potential downfall of your B&B business can be an untapped consequence. Hence, ignoring zoning laws should never be considered an option when you're embarking on the B&B journey.

4.3. Understanding and Navigating Zoning Regulations

To start understanding relevant zoning laws, a good starting point is your local planning or zoning department. These departments are typically located in your municipal or county buildings.

Local ordinances often detail land use and structures allowed in specific locations. They also generally outline procedures for seeking zoning changes and detailing penalties for violations. A checklist for understanding zoning laws should encompass the following aspects:

1. Access to where zoning maps and regulations are located

2. Thorough perusal of these maps and regulations

3. Locate your property on the zoning map

4. Identify the zone in which your property falls

5. Read about the uses that are allowed as a matter of right, special uses, and prohibited uses in your zoning group.

Sometimes, a property may be used for an incompatible reason if the property owner obtains a special-use permit. It's then good to remember that these permits are generally granted sparingly and typically involve a considerable level of bureaucracy and delay.

4.4. Seeking Legal Advice

Even with a good understanding of zoning laws, the nuances involved might overwhelm you. Thus, it's highly advisable to seek professional legal assistance when it comes to understanding zoning regulations. A professional can guide you through the sometimes labyrinthine maze of rules, regulations, and exceptions. They can also make you aware of any future developments, such as a zoning change that is up for discussion in the city council which could potentially affect you.

In summary, understanding zoning laws and regulations is an essential aspect of starting and operating a profitable B&B. Even though it may seem intimidating at first, with the right resources and approach, you can easily navigate this legal labyrinth. A well-informed and zoning law-compliant B&B will not only secure you from unforeseen legal and financial ramifications but will also work wonders in laying the foundation of a thriving and successful B&B business. Now that you are well-suited with the knowledge of zoning laws and regulations, you are one step closer to opening the doors of your very own cozy B&B.

Chapter 5. Securing Funding: Financial Considerations and Strategies

Converting a dream into a reality often requires resources, and one of the most critical resources is funding. Investigating and securing financial resources for your bed-and-breakfast enterprise can be a daunting task, but it doesn't have to be. With careful research, prudent planning, understanding of your financial needs, and strategic maneuvering, you can secure the funds necessary to launch and operate your B&B.

5.1. Assess Your Personal Financial Situation

Start with your current financial situation. You need to have an honest look at your personal finances. Begin with calculating your net worth – your assets minus your liabilities. This exercise will provide an insight into your financial standing and readiness for taking on this venture. Understanding your cash flow and identifying areas where you can cut costs to save is crucial at this stage.

Remember, your personal savings and resources can play a fundamental role in financing your B&B venture during its early stages. However, this isn't always a viable or recommended path. Diversifying your funding sources is vital for mitigating risks and maintaining financial stability. Hence, while you might need to dip into your personal savings, it's recommended to seek external funding as well.

5.2. Estimating Startup Costs for Your B&B

You must accurately estimate the startup costs for your venture. These costs typically include purchasing or renting the property, renovation and remodeling, furnishing, initial operating expenses, and emergency funds.

When estimating renovation costs, consult with a local contractor who is familiar with older homes (if you're considering a historical structure), or those who have experience in converting properties into B&Bs.

Don't forget to factor in the marketing and advertising budget, permit costs, and initial staffing salaries. A contingency fund for unexpected costs is also recommended. Once you've calculated the total startup costs, you'll have a clear target sum for your funding efforts.

5.3. Evaluate Potential Funding Sources

Bank Loans: Traditional bank loans can be one of the first avenues to explore. You will need a comprehensive business plan and personal financial statement to apply for a bank loan. If the bank perceives your venture as carrying high risk, you could consider an SBA (Small Business Administration) loan. These loans have government backing, which lowers the risk for banks.

Private Investors: If traditional banking routes aren't available or favorable, consider finding private investors. These individuals or groups may be interested in partial ownership of your business in exchange for their investment.

Crowdfunding: Platforms like Kickstarter and Indiegogo offer entrepreneurs a chance to tap into the public's funds by sharing their vision and goals. But remember, successful crowdfunding requires a compelling story and attractive rewards for backers.

5.4. Successfully Applying for a Business Loan

Understand the key terms and considerations that loan officials look for in a potential borrower. These include:

- Credit Score: A healthy credit score is a prerequisite.
- Collateral: Most banks demand collateral to secure the loan.
- Cash Flow Projections: Prove through your business plan that your B&B will generate sufficient cash flow.

Use simple and clear narratives in your business plan, convincingly showcasing your drive, dedication, and competence.

5.5. Navigating the Funding Jigsaw

Getting your financial footing right is a multifaceted task. Between your personal savings, bank loans, private investors, and crowdfunding, there are numerous funding pieces you need to fit together in your funding puzzle. However, keep in mind that the financial landscape is constantly changing.

Collaborate with financial advisors and experienced entrepreneurs to navigate this jigsaw and find the best possible solution for your financial needs. Your strategy should also be dynamic, ready to adapt to changing circumstances and opportunities as they present themselves.

Securing funding for your B&B venture is a crucial step in turning your dream into reality. With diligent planning, accurate cost estimation, fruitful negotiations, and a deep understanding of potential funding sources, your financial foundation will be as welcoming as the cozy room and home-baked muffins awaiting your first guest.

Chapter 6. Property Transformation: From House to Inviting Inn

The first step in establishing your own bed and breakfast is transforming an existing house into an inviting inn. At the heart of this process is a continuum of essential tasks - market analysis, renovation planning, understanding local compliance, effective remodeling, and creating an enticing décor.

6.1. Market Analysis and Property Selection

Insightful market analysis and property selection set the foundation of your bed and breakfast business. Before purchasing a property, thoroughly understand the local market. Consider factors such as tourist attractions, peak visitor seasons, and the competition posed by other B&Bs. It is also crucial to take the preferences of your target demographic into account. What style of house is likely to appeal to them – classical, traditional, or modern?

Seek professional help when deciding on location. Real estate agents, in particular, will have a good understanding of property trends and will be able to provide valuable advice. It is important to consider properties that offer adequate space for guest rooms along with private living quarters for you and your family.

6.2. Renovation Planning

With the property selected, the next step is to develop a detailed renovation plan. This will involve making sound decisions regarding the usage of space, the division of rooms, the choice of exteriors, and the selection of interiors. You might consider hiring an architect or an interior designer who specializes in B&B transformations for the best results.

Start each room design with a list of needs, potential room arrangement schemes, and design specifications. Your guest rooms should provide a comfortable and appealing environment to foster a homelike atmosphere.

6.3. Understanding Local Compliance

Before any renovation work begins, it's important to ensure you are in compliance with local zoning laws and building codes. These laws may dictate the permissible extent of renovations, how many guest rooms you can have, whether you can serve food, signage allowances, and many other logistical elements.

Fire safety is another crucial aspect encompassed within building code regulations. It influences factors such as the construction and layout of rooms, the number and type of exits, and the installation of smoke detectors and sprinklers. Consultation with regulatory agencies and legal professionals is vital to ensure you meet all legal requirements.

6.4. Effective Remodeling

Renovation doesn't merely involve enhancing aesthetic appeal; it's about creating an environment that will make guests feel at home, relaxed, and choose your B&B over other accommodation options in the area.

Kitchen upgrades are crucial for your B&B as the quality of breakfast you serve is a large part of the experience. In addition, it's essential to focus on your guest rooms, bathrooms, and common areas. Install comfortable beds, invest in quality linens, and ensure that the bathroom fixtures are up to date and visually pleasing.

Common areas, such as the living room and the garden, need to foster relaxation and conversation among your guests. Consider adding a fireplace, comfortable sofas, a library, or a coffee station, depending on available space.

6.5. Creating an Inviting Décor

Finally, perfect the ambiance of your B&B through thoughtful décor choices. The initial impression of the decor and style of your B&B can often be the determining factor of whether or not a guest chooses to book.

Consider the color palette of your interiors, the type of furniture, lighting options, wall décor, and other small touches that go a long way in making an environment more welcoming. Each room should reflect a unique charm without deviating too much from your overall style statement.

The right ambiance can define what makes your bed and breakfast exclusive and helps project it as an inviting inn. The ultimate goal is to create a space that acts as a home-away-from-home, offering guests the right blend of comfort, intimacy, and luxury.

In conclusion, transforming property into an inviting bed and breakfast requires a well-planned strategy that combines astute market insights, careful planning, adherence to local rules, practical remodeling, and tasteful décor. While this process can be intense, remember that it forms the foundation of your B&B venture, a stepping stone to a profitable entrepreneurial journey filled with fresh-baked muffins, bubbling conversations, warmth, and a unique guest experience that keeps your guests coming back for more.

Chapter 7. Mastering the Hospitality: Hiring and Training Your Team

First impressions are everything in hospitality, and a well-trained, approachable, and proficient team can be that difference between a good bed and breakfast and a great one. But what does it take to build such a team? Understanding who to hire and how to train them is central to this endeavor.

7.1. The Hiring Process

To assemble a team that reflects the value and charm of your bed and breakfast, you need to define what roles your business requires and the skills applicable to them. Common roles in a B&B include: front desk personnel, housekeeping staff, kitchen staff, and maintenance personnel.

You'll want to write detailed job descriptions for each position, outlining key responsibilities, expected duties, desirable skills, and any other specific requirements pertaining to the role. This not only aids the clarity of job advertisements but also provides a common understanding between you and your staff members about their job requirements.

When setting up your hiring process, be aware that while qualifications and prior experience are worthwhile measures of potential performance, they aren't the whole picture. Emphasize the importance of soft skills such as communication, reliability, attentiveness, and a general jovial demeanor, given that your staff will frequently interact with guests and represent your brand.

7.2. Training Basics

After you've found your dream team, the next step is ensuring they can perform their tasks competently and manage customer interactions positively. Effective training programs encompass both the technical and customer service aspects of their roles.

Technical proficiency is role dependent and should cover every major task your staff will undertake. Housekeepers, for example, should know the standards for cleanliness, the correct use of cleaning materials and equipment, safety protocols, and so on. Front desk personnel, on the other hand, need to master administrative tasks, bookings, cancellations, and other front-of-house operations.

While technical skills are essential, your B&B's charm and appeal depend largely on how guests perceive their interactions with your personnel. Soft skills training is vital, placing focus on effective communication, conflict resolution, problem-solving, multi-tasking, and display of professionalism and warmth during interaction with guests.

7.3. Implementing Standard Operating Procedures

Standard Operating Procedures (SOPs) ensure that your staff performs their duties uniformly and to your expectations. They allow everyone to be on the same page about what exactly their jobs entail, regardless of who's on shift. This generates more consistent and reliable service and operations for your B&B.

SOPs should cover a set of written instructions for all roles, outlining each step of every critical task, such as daily opening and closing procedures, guest check-in and check-out processes, food preparation, housekeeping routines, and emergency handling.

Regular updates should be made as needed, ensuring your SOPs evolve along with your business, but do remember to communicate any changes directly to all staff members.

7.4. Continuous Professional Development

Creating an environment where continuous learning is encouraged may help keep your staff happy and motivated. The hospitality industry constantly evolves with innovations in technology and changes in customer trends, and it would greatly benefit your B&B if your staff are kept up to date with these developments.

Investing in your team by providing regular training and development opportunities can keep them engaged and devoted. This can range from workshops and seminars on new food trends for kitchen staff, to attending industry conferences, to online courses for enhancing their customer service skills.

7.5. Cultivating a Positive Work Culture

Finally, successful training is not just about learning the right skills but being in the right environment to flourish. Fostering a workplace that practices open communication, respects diversity, prioritizes staff wellbeing, and acknowledges good work helps create a positive work culture where your employees feel appreciated and committed to doing their best.

Remember, the hospitality you extend to your guests is as good as the hospitality you extend to your staff.

In conclusion, hiring and training an outstanding team is an ongoing effort. It requires thoughtful planning and consideration from the hiring stages to regular continued development and establishment of a supportive work culture. Equipped with these insights, you can now confidently make strides towards mastering the hospitality in your charming bed and breakfast business.

Chapter 8. Creating a Signature Guest Experience

Creating a signature guest experience is not just about exceptional customer service; it is about creating that unique mark that sets your bed and breakfast apart from others. This should be a blend of personalized hospitality, thoughtfulness, attention to detail, and creating an atmosphere where guests feel cherished and at home.

8.1. The Foundation of a Memorable Stay

A great guest experience starts with the foundations. The key is knowing your guests well and providing thoughtful additions that cater to their individual preferences and needs.

Think about what specifically you want your guests to remember about their stay. Is it the welcoming atmosphere, the top-notch service, or the uniquely-decorated rooms? Express your brand's identity through these foundational elements, and guests will remember not just the lodging, but the entire enjoyable experience.

8.2. The Art of Personalized Hospitality

One of the advantages of a bed and breakfast over larger establishments is the opportunity for a close personal relationship with your guests.

Start by personalizing their stay. Get to know your guests' reasons for visiting and their preferences even before they arrive. A short pre-arrival questionnaire can work wonders here. You can email this to your upcoming guests and get a head start in understanding their preferences.

Take note of guests' preferences, remember their names, and recognize repeated guests. Use these details to provide tailored recommendations, such as suggesting activities and local attractions, and customizing rooms according to preferences.

8.3. Thoughtful Touches

It's the small thoughtful touches that often leave a lasting impression. These could include a welcome basket with local products, a handwritten welcome note, or a free upgrade for a milestone celebration.

Consider offering in-room extras, like a selection of books, fluffy robes, luxurious bath products, or a guide to local attractions. These small gestures enhance the guest experience and add a touch of luxury to their stay.

Don't forget about the importance of knowledgeable staff. Having employees who can engage in friendly conversation, offer detailed information about the local area, and respond to requests quickly and efficiently will make a significant positive impact on your guests' experience.

8.4. Designing Spaces for Comfort

Your bed and breakfast should not only be a place for your guests to sleep but also a place where they can relax, unwind, and feel at home. This means paying attention to both the communal areas and individual rooms.

Communal areas should invite guests to socialize and relax. A cozy lounge area with a log fire, a garden with seating, or a library filled with books can offer spaces for visitors to feel at home. The breakfast room should be inviting, comfortable, and meticulously clean.

Individual rooms should also be well thought out. The decor should reflect the identity of your B&B without favoring any extreme design that could polarize your clientele. Ensure room functionality with plenty of storage, well-placed lighting, and comfortable beds.

8.5. Creating an Unforgettable Breakfast Experience

The breakfast in a bed and breakfast is a primary part of the guest experience. It's more than just a meal, it provides an opportunity to showcase your B&B's uniqueness while providing a social hub for guests. A beautiful, delicious, and locally sourced breakfast can leave your guests with remarkable memories.

Offer a variety of options to cater to all taste buds and dietary requirements. Guests will appreciate having options; from the full English experience to continental delights, or a fruity, healthy alternative.

Remember, presentation is everything! Serving the meals on quality tableware, arranging the food appealingly, and offering attention to small details can significantly enhance the guest's breakfast experience.

8.6. Embracing Technology

Technology has become an integral part of the hospitality industry. From booking systems to in-room entertainment, guests today expect some level of digital experience. However, it should not take away from the warmth and personal service B&Bs are known for.

Consider incorporating smart features into your rooms, like USB outlets or smart TVs. Have a strong Wi-Fi connection and make sure it's available throughout your property. An easy online booking system can also enhance guests' first experience with your B&B before they even arrive.

On one hand, offering an advanced digital experience can impress, but don't forget it's the blend of traditional hospitality mixed with these conveniences that create a memorable experience.

By implementing these factors into your mindset and actions, you'll create an unforgettable guest experience that will serve as the cornerstone of your bed and breakfast success.

Chapter 9. The Art of Crafting Memorable Breakfast Menus

In order to ensure your Bed and Breakfast establishment stands out in a crowded marketplace, a one-of-a-kind breakfast menu is just the ticket. Offering your patrons uniquely delectable meals each morning is undeniably a critical way to ensure repeat business, and garner rave reviews that fetch more guests. The following chapters explore this art in depth, peppered with helpful advice, insightful tips, and practical suggestions to aid your efforts.

9.1. Understanding your Audience

Before we delve into the finer details of crafting an unforgettable breakfast menu, the first crucial step is understanding your audience. Your menu should cater to the varied tastes and dietary preferences of your potential guests, ensuring everyone starts their day on a delightful note. To do this, consider creating a short survey for your guests to fill out prior to their arrival. This could include questions about their favorite breakfast foods, any dietary restrictions, and their preferred serving time. Use this data to gain insight into your customer's likes and dislikes, which will help tailor your menu to their palates.

9.2. Balancing Nutritional and Decadent Options

A memorable breakfast menu strikes a healthy balance between rich, decadent options and lighter, heath-focused choices. Offering a variety of dishes will cater to guests with various dietary preferences and restrictions. As a host, your job is to offer a choice, letting your guests select what suits them best. For instance, fresh fruit salads, oatmeal, and granolas would appeal to health-conscious guests while pancakes, bacon, and eggs would satisfy those looking for a traditional breakfast spread. It's all about finding the right balance to please every palate.

9.3. Seasonality and Locally-Sourced Ingredients

Using seasonal, locally-sourced produce not only enhances the quality and flavor of your meals, but also underscores a commitment to sustainable practices. Visit local farmer's markets, establish relationships with local farms, or even grow your own ingredients in a kitchen garden. The freshness of your ingredients will shine through in your meals and contribute to a memorable breakfast experience.

9.4. Breakfast Specialties and Unique Offerings

Stand out from your competition by offering breakfast specialties that no other B&B offers. These could be dishes native to your area, family recipes, or unique creations of your own design. Creativity and innovation on the breakfast table can transform a regular stay into an extraordinary experience.

9.5. Catering to Dietary Restrictions

In today's world, a B&B owner must be knowledgeable about various dietary restrictions, such as gluten-free, vegan, vegetarian, dairy-free, and low-carb diets, among others. Including a few options for these dietary restrictions in your menu is not simply considerate, it becomes an additional selling point for your establishment. When a guest with dietary restrictions sees that they are catered for, they feel seen, valued, and cared for, and that's an experience they are likely to share with others.

9.6. Presentation and Ambiance

A memorable breakfast experience isn't just about great food. The ambiance, table setting, and presentation play significant roles in creating a memorable experience. Try using aesthetically pleasing tableware, arranging the food in an appealing way, and ensuring your breakfast room has a cozy and inviting feel. These subtle details can transform an ordinary breakfast into an extraordinary one.

9.7. Consistency and Variety

While it's important to maintain a certain degree of consistency, ensuring guests know what they can expect, introducing a bit of variety from time to time keeps things fresh and exciting. Rotate certain dishes on your menu on a weekly or monthly basis, depending on the frequency of repeat guests.

Finally, remember, running a successful bed and breakfast is much more than managing a business. It's about providing a warm, welcoming experience that people will remember and cherish. An exceptional breakfast is a vital part of creating such an experience. It has the potential to leave a lasting impression on your guests, encouraging them to return and recommend your establishment to others. By honing your skills in crafting memorable, mouth-watering breakfast menus, and coupling this with warm hospitality, your B&B is sure to flourish.

Chapter 10. Marketing Your B&B: Strategies for Success

An effective marketing strategy is the linchpin of success in the competitive realm of bed and breakfast establishments. Success isn't merely about providing a homely ambiance and serving lip-smacking breakfasts; it requires you to make your B&B visible, alluring, and accessible to both local and global potential guests. This chapter uncovers the most effective techniques to do just that.

10.1. Identifying Your Unique Selling Proposition

The first crucial step in marketing your B&B is pinpointing what imbues your establishment with a unique allure. This is called your Unique Selling Proposition (USP) and it sets you apart in the teeming landscape of B&Bs.

To identify your USP, ask yourself:

- What makes my B&B different from others?
- Does my B&B have any exclusive architectural features?
- Is it located in a unique geographical location?
- Do I serve any signature dishes or exclusive local delicacies?

Finally, utilize this identified USP as the beacon of all your marketing campaigns.

10.2. Taking the Digital Road: Website and SEO

In the digital age, your B&B must have an online presence to reach out to the digital-savvy guest. The first footprint on digital soil is your website.

Ensure your website is well-designed, incredibly navigable, and mobile-compatible. Photographs of your B&B should be professionally taken to ensure top quality. Include clear, articulate descriptions of your amenities, along with prices. Your contact details should be explicitly displayed.

To drive traffic to your website, invest time in Search Engine Optimization (SEO). Incorporate relevant keywords and phrases. Used by potential guests when they conduct online searches, these will pull your website to the top in Search Engine Result Pages (SERP). Sharing your USP through a compelling storytelling approach will make a significant difference.

10.3. Using the Power of Social Media

Social media platforms can efficiently boost your B&B's visibility and allure. Instagram, with its emphasis on visuals, is a remarkably useful platform where you can share stunning photographs of your B&B. Facebook can be leveraged to connect with a broader audience and share special offers, events, or promotions. Twitter, on the other hand, is a great place for quick updates and interactive conversations.

Engaging regularly on social media establishes an honest image of your B&B in a way that traditional marketing sometimes can't achieve. This friendly digital persona will draw in guests who value transparency and connection.

10.4. Registering with Online Booking Sites

Online booking websites (like Airbnb, Booking.com, Expedia, etc.) can widen your reach dramatically. They not only expose your B&B to a global audience but also provide easy booking facilities.

Regularly update your listing, respond swiftly and politely to enquiries, and sincerely consider guest feedback to improve your services.

10.5. The Role of Guest Reviews

Authentic guest reviews are pure marketing gold. They do not just show potential guests what to expect; positive reviews provide concrete validation of your B&B's excellence.

Encourage guests to leave a review after their stay. Respond to each review to showcase your commitment to guest satisfaction.

10.6. Developing Collaborative Arrangements

Strategic collaborations with local restaurants, stores, and tour guides can be a rewarding marketing strategy. You can create unique package deals with these collaborators. These packages add to your B&B's value proposition and attract guests looking for an immersive experience.

10.7. Leveraging Offline Advertising

Although digital marketing strategies are powerful, offline advertising methods shouldn't be neglected. Newspaper ads, local radio spots, billboards, flyers, brochures, or even word-of-mouth can be effective in driving traffic to your B&B, especially within the local community.

Developing a strong marketing strategy entails a good understanding of who your guests are and what they value, identifying your selling points, and leveraging both online and offline channels to reach out to your potential guests. Done right, marketing can ensure a steady stream of bookings, increased profits, and the achievement of your B&B dream.

Chapter 11. Maintaining Profitability and Overcoming Challenges

Operating a bed and breakfast inn can be a dream come true for many aspiring entrepreneurs. However, maintaining profitability and overcoming challenges calls for a unique set of skills, expertise, and tools. Along with the pleasure of welcoming guests from around the world comes the responsibility of running a successful small business—keeping your B&B profitable while working through various challenges. Let's explore how you can accomplish that.

11.1. Understanding Your Expenses

The first step towards maintaining profitability is having a firm grasp on your operational costs. B&B's, like any business, have both fixed and variable expenses. Here's a rough breakdown:

1. Fixed Costs:
   - Insurance
   - Property taxes
   - Mortgage or rent
   - Depreciation
   - Utilities

2. Variable Costs:
   - Food and beverages
   - Cleaning supplies
   - Linens and toiletries
   - Advertising and marketing

- ◦ Incidentals

Understanding where your money is being spent allows you to make conscious decisions about what may need to be adjusted. Review these expenses regularly and look for areas where you might be able to cut costs.

11.2. Managing Guest Expectations and Experience

A huge part of sustaining profits in the B&B industry lies in managing your guests' expectations and experiences. The key here is to consistently exceed expectations. Make sure your online presence accurately represents your establishment. From your website to your social media feeds, make sure everything is updated and clearly shows what guests can expect from their stay.

Remember, keeping your guests pleased is easier and more cost-effective than finding new patrons. Asking returning guests to write reviews or testimonials can also help attract new visitors.

11.3. Offering Unique, Irresistible Experiences

The hospitality industry thrives on uniqueness. Guests often opt for B&Bs because they're searching for unique stays. Reflect this in the experiences you offer, from tastefully-furnished rooms to locally-sourced meals and featured activities or packages.

Come up with packages that cater to a diverse range of interests. Wine tastings, cooking classes, local tours, or wellness retreats; all these can make your B&B more enticing to potential guests and increase the likelihood of repeat patronage.

11.4. Proactive Marketing and Networking

Solid marketing can keep your B&B filled and profitable. Utilizing online platforms and local tourism networks can improve your visibility. Ensure you have a deep understanding of your target market; their wants, needs, and travel habits. Leverage online platforms for advertising and offers that cater to your target market.

Local networking is also crucial. Build connections with local businesses and fellow B&B owners. This not only helps you stay updated on industry trends but can create opportunities for collaboration that benefits everyone involved.

11.5. Overcoming Common B&B Challenges

Like any business, running a B&B comes with its challenges. Here are a few common issues you might encounter, along with solutions to overcome them.

1. Low Season Slump: All hospitality businesses face slow seasons. This challenge is about mitigating the impact of lower footfall. Consider creative strategies like off-season packages or hosting local events.

2. Maintenance Costs: Keeping a property in top condition is crucial for B&Bs, but it also adds to costs. Regular preventive maintenance can help prevent major repairs and keep costs down.

3. The 24/7 Responsibility: The nature of a B&B operation means you're almost always on call. To avoid burnout, it's necessary to establish clear boundaries and get help when needed.

4. Dealing with Difficult Guests: Not all guests will be easy to please.

Develop strategies to deal with difficult situations professionally and compassionarily, ensuring your business' reputation remains positive.

Pursuing your dream of running a bed and breakfast inn requires more than just a love for hospitality. It demands careful financial management, exceptional guest experiences, and a proactive approach to overcoming challenges. With these tools at your disposal, you're well on your way to creating a successful, profitable B&B that will stand the test of time. Balancing these aspects effectively is the key to long-term success and profitability in the B&B industry. Keep innovating, stay connected with your guests, and remember, the magic lies in the details.